M000301501

TO HELL
with the
DEVIL

———— ❧ ————

*It's Time to Blow
the Lid off Lucifer's Coffin*

Gary Randall Wallace

ISBN 978-1-0980-8988-7 (paperback)
ISBN 978-1-0980-8991-7 (digital)

Copyright © 2023 by Gary Randall Wallace

All rights reserved. No part of this publication may be reproduced, distributed, or transmitted in any form or by any means, including photocopying, recording, or other electronic or mechanical methods without the prior written permission of the publisher. For permission requests, solicit the publisher via the address below.

Christian Faith Publishing, Inc.
832 Park Avenue
Meadville, PA 16335
www.christianfaithpublishing.com

Printed in the United States of America

To my wife and bestfriend Lillian
To my twin brother Larry Wallace—both of us,
Servants of the Lord over 40 years

Yes, you heard me right—Lucifer's coffin. Remember that song in the *Wizard of Oz*. "Dingdong, dingdong, the wicked witch, the wicked witch is dead." Well, he's been dead for over 2,500 years. This truth, no doubt, will upset many theologians, devil worshipers, Masons, Satanists, and the many Luciferians throughout all the secret societies, including the Vatican. It is time the truth be told. It's certainly not going to make me popular. But the sheep of the Lord that hear his voice, they will indeed rejoice. No more big daddy devil to impede their ability to be overcomers. So come hell or high water, I'm going to tell it.

My source is from the truth itself, the Bible, and historical fact. You will not find any endorsements from any famous or well-known people. I'm certainly not famous, and I certainly don't know anyone famous, evangelical, or otherwise. I'm probably of average intelligence and can barely get my pants on the morning.

I'm just someone that has sought the truth for over forty years in the Scriptures. What I'm going to reveal here is just good common sense, which in today's world is in a very low commodity, especially in Washington, DC, and many institutions of the so-called *higher learning*.

I'm going to give you a little bit of my background. I think you might find it interesting, as I'm not even supposed to be here. It is only by a miracle from the Lord that I exist at all. At the age of fifteen, my friend's sister squeezed my right bicep and gave me a rather strange look. She said, "That muscle seems awfully hard." She went to my mother and said that I should probably go see a doctor and have it x-rayed, which we did. The x-ray revealed a large tumor the size of a softball. Of course as a kid I just assumed it was a large muscle and proud of it. The doctor said it would have to be removed because it was malignant. What I was not told by the doctor, William Grannis, was that the arm would be removed from the shoulder, and I may live to be twenty-one years old. In fact I was never told this until some five or six years later. As my mother tells it, after she received the bad news, she was walking down the hall past my bedroom where I was asleep and began to cry. She said suddenly a voice spoke to her and said, "Daughter, where's your faith?" Two weeks later or so, just before the surgery, a Dr. Thatcher from Chicago was on vacation and decided to visit the Stanford Hospital facilities. He was the first doctor to successfully do a bone transplant. And because Stanford University and hospital was world known, he decided to make a visit.

When Dr. Thatcher arrived, it was buzzing all over the hospital. It was as if God had arrived. With Dr. Thatcher's instructions, and the Lord (Dr. Grannis told my mother that there was a strong presence directing him through the whole operation) he directed Dr. Grannis through the procedure. It took four operations through four consecutive years to complete. The right humerus with the tumor attached was completely removed. A long pin was attached to my elbow and shoulder, and bone grafts from my pelvis and chins were tied to the pin with wire. In the last surgery, a titanium plate with six screws completed the surgeries. Apparently, in the old days, they simply open the arm up and scrape the tumor off the bone, but many years later, it would return again. I was not the first but the second to have a successful bone transplant. This was 1962.

I'm very thankful to the Lord for saving my life and sparing me for this very reason—to tell the world what has been said in his Word over and over again. "There is no God besides me. For there were no gods but the work of men's hands, wood and stone, which neither see nor hear nor eat nor smell" (Deut. 4:28). So why don't we start at Mount Carmel in the eighteenth chapter of 1 Kings, where the great prophet Elijah confronted eight hundred prophets of Baal. This is in the Bible, just in case some of you have never read it.

So why do men and preachers want to make Lucifer a god? And a doctrine that is entirely made up in the minds of *man*, the real devil and Satan. Uh-oh! I guess let that last part slip. I can almost feel the stones whizzing past my head. We will deal with this provocative statement later.

Let's begin by reading 1 Kings chapter 18, starting at verse 17.

> And it came to pass, when Ahab [king of Israel] saw Elijah that Ahab said unto him, Art thou he that troubleth Israel? And he answered I have not troubled Israel; but thou, and thy father's house, and that ye have forsaken the commandments of the Lord, and thou has followed Baalim. Now therefore send, and gather to me all Israel unto mount Carmel, and the prophets of Baal 450, and the prophets of the Grove 400, which eat at Jezebels [the king's wife] table. So Ahab sent unto all the children of *Israel* unto mount Carmel, and Elijah came unto all the people, and said, how long halt ye between two opinions. If the Lord be God, follow him; but if Baal, then follow him; and the people answered him not a word. Then said Elijah unto the people. I, even I only, remain a prophet of the Lord; but Baal's prophets are 450 men. Let them therefore give us two bullocks; and let them choose one bullock for themselves, and cut it in pieces, and lay it on wood, and put no fire under; and I will dress the other bullock, and lay it on wood, and put no fire under; and call ye on the name of your gods, and I will call on the name of the Lord; and the God that answers by fire, let him be God. And all the people answered and said, it is well spoken. And Elijah said unto the profits of Baal, choose you one bullock for yourselves, and dress it first; for you are many; and call on the name of your gods,

but put no fire under. And they took the bullock which was given them, and they dressed it, and called on the name of Baal from morning even until noon, saying, O Baal, hear us. But there was no voice, nor any that answered. And they leaped upon the altar which was made. And it came to pass at noon, that Elijah mocked them, and said, cry aloud; for he is a God; either he is talking, or he is pursuing, or he is on a journey, or perhaps he is sleeping, and must be awakened. And they cried aloud, and cut themselves after their manner with knives and lancets, till the blood gushed out upon them. And it came to pass, when that day was passed, and he prophesied until the time of the offering of the evening sacrifice, that there was neither voice, nor any to answer, nor any that regarded.

(Apparently he was able to cause a rebellion in heaven and steal a third of God's angels in the process, which is taught in many churches today, but Elijah must have scared the hell out of him.)

Now maybe you are beginning to see the picture. Where was the god Baal or Lucifer, or Satan, or how about the devil? Since they all sleep in the same bed together. It is quite obvious that he simply didn't exist, (or at least in a godly form.) Or maybe he was just a coward, and didn't want to show up. He's sure missed a great opportunity to show his power and his greatness. Wow, that was sure a whole lot of bloodletting for nothing. Now you are probably asking yourselves, Is this guy saying there is no devil or Satan? No, what I am saying is that the devil and Satan are not angels that fell somewhere out of heaven. And not only fell out of heaven but took along one-third of God's angels. This is one of the most misinterpreted doctrines ever preached. And this is something that we're going to correct by the only way it can be corrected, through the Scriptures. And we will address this also in a later chapter.

Let's continue from verse 30.

And Elijah said unto all the people, come near unto me. And all the people came near unto him. And he repaired the altar of the Lord that was broken down. And Elijah took 12 stones, according to the number of the tribes of the sons of Jacob, unto whom the word of the Lord came, saying, Israel shall be thy name; and with the stones he built an altar in the name of the Lord; and he made a trench about the altar, as great as would contain two measures of seed. And he put the wood in order, and cut the Bullock in pieces, and laid him on the wood, and said, "Fill four barrels with water, and pour it on the burnt sacrifice and on the wood." And he said, "Do it the second time." And he did it the second time and he said, "Do it the third time." And they did it the third time. And the water ran round about the altar; and he filled the trench also with water. And it came to pass at the time of the offering of the evening sacrifice, that Elijah the prophet, came near, and said, Lord God of Abraham, Isaac, and of Israel, let it be known this day that thou art God in Israel, and that I am thy servant, and that I have done all these things at thy word. Hear me, oh Lord, hear me, that this people may know that thou art the Lord God, and that thou hast turned their heart back again. Then the fire of the Lord fell, and consumed the burnt sacrifice, and the wood, and the stones, and the dust, and licked up the water that was in the trench. And when all the people saw it, they fell on their faces; and they said the Lord, he is the God; the Lord, he is the God.

In the Old Testament, God declares innumerable times, "There is no God besides me." One of my favorite chapters is Isaiah 44. And it is to me, almost comical. Now I am not going to quote this whole chapter. I'm simply going to paraphrase it. The Lord speaks to Israel concerning their idol worship. "You go out into the forest and cut down a tree. You make a fire and warm yourselves, then you bake your bread, and with the rest of the wood you carve yourself a god and bow down and worship it. It can neither see nor walk nor talk nor speak. For thou art brainless." Forgive me, I had to throw in that last sentence myself. What is amazing to me is that this idol worship is just as alive and well today as it was back then. Let me quote you a scripture from the Bible, the book of Romans chapter 1 beginning at verse 20 through 25.

> For the invisible things of him from the creation of the world are clearly seen, being understood by the things that are made, even his eternal power and Godhead; so that they are without excuse; because that, when they knew God, they glorified him not as God, neither were thankful; but became vain in their imaginations and their foolish heart was darkened. Professing themselves to be wise they became fools, and changed the glory of the incorruptible God into an image made like to corruptible man, and to birds, and four-footed beasts, and creeping things. Wherefore God also gave them up to uncleanness through the lust of their own hearts, to dishonor their own bodies between themselves; who changed the truth of God into a lie, and worshiped and served the creature more than the creator who is blessed forever. Amen.

ISAIAH 14

As to the fallen angel Lucifer of Yeshayahu (Isaiah) 14:12 it is a Christian misunderstanding of the text. Hailail, the name in the text, and not Lucifer (there is no Lucifer anywhere in Hebrew Scripture), is the morning star... VENUS. People would rise at dawn and see one lonely star in the sky, and some assume, in error, that the star had fallen from the Heavens, and the myth of the rebelling angel was born. Hailail is Venus, which can still be seen on certain mornings long after all the other stars have tucked themselves away.

The word *Lucifer* is mentioned only once in the entire Bible. And that is in the chapter of Isaiah 14. The Hebrew or Aramaic word for Lucifer is *hay-lale*, meaning "brightness, to shine, to make a show, to boast." So were talking about a person who is boastful and a showoff, who thinks himself to be better than everybody else. Let's look at what King Nebuchadnezzar says in Daniel 4 and verse 30. "And the king spoke, and said, is not this great Babylon, that I have built for the house of the kingdom by the might of MY power, and for the honor of MY Majesty?" I would say, this sounds like a very boastful person like Lucifer in Isaiah 14. So this is not someone who was up in heaven and caused a great rebellion. First of all, there is no sin in heaven—at least not in third heaven, the dwelling place of the Lord God. And if we read first Samuel 15:23, it says, "For rebellion is as the sin of witchcraft, and stubbornness is as iniquity, and idolatry." So if there was a rebellion in heaven, there had to be sin, and if sin, then death. Even if you're not learned or have much knowledge of the Scripture, you will agree that nobody dies in heaven. In Romans 6:23 it says this, "the wages of sin is death, but the gift of God is eternal life." And it's not talking about the flesh because we all die, it's talking about the soul, and you'll find throughout the Bible scriptures that talk about the death of the soul. So we have a problem with this myth that is preached out here about a rebellion that took place in heaven. So let us go to Isaiah 14 and begin in verse 4. "And that thou shall take up this proverb against the King of Babylon, and say, how hath the oppressor ceased! The Golden city ceased!" The keyword in this verse is *proverb*. In the original Hebrew, this word is *maw-shawl*—in some original sense of superiority in mental action, probably a pithy maxim, usually of a metaphorical nature; hence, a simile, such as an adage, poem, discourse, and byword, like, *parable, proverb. Proverb* is the same word *parable* in the New Testament. The original Greek word for parable is *parabole*, "a fictitious narrative of common life conveying a moral." So from the very beginning, this chapter is a fictitious narrative of a metaphorical nature. No more, no less.

Let's continue to verse 5 and the rest of the story—or should I say, proverb. "The Lord hath broken the staff of the wicked, and the scepter of the rulers." Verse 6, "He who smote the people in wrath with a continual stroke, he that ruled the nations [I don't ever recall in history Lucifer ruling a kingdom on earth, but Nebuchadnezzer, king of Babylon, did, whom this whole chapter is addressing in verse 4] in anger, is persecuted, and none hindereth." Verse 7, "The whole earth is at rest, and is quiet; they break forth into singing." Verse 8, "Yea, the fir trees rejoice at thee, and the Cedars of Lebanon, saying, since thou art laid down, no feller is come up against us." Before we go any further, let's look Jeremiah 27:7: "And all nations shall serve him [King Nebuchadnezzar], his son [Merdoach], and his son's son [Belshazzar] until the very time his land come: and then many nations and great kings shall serve themselves of him." So verses 5 and 6 of Isaiah 14 says exactly what Jeremiah 27:7 says about King Nebuchadnezzar, his son and grandson, and that is that he was destroyed eventually by many nation and kings. Verse 9–11, "And hell from beneath is moved for thee two meet thee at thy coming; it stirred up the dead for thee, even all the chief ones of the earth; it has raised up from their thrones all the kings of the nations. All they shall speak and say unto thee, art thou also become weak as we? Art thou become like unto us? Thy pomp is brought down to the grave, and the noise of thy viles. The worm is spread under thee, and the worms cover thee."

Now let's stop here for a moment. These verses are simply saying King Nebuchadnezzar conquered the whole known world and nothing could stop him except the God of heaven. And hell came in the form of Persia and stirred up other nations to eventually destroy Babylon. So all your glory has gone down to the grave. And the worms will devourer your flesh just like any man that was ever born. The next verse, verse 12, is one of the most controversial verses in all of Scripture.

"How art thou fallen from heaven, O Lucifer, son of the morning how art thou cut down to the ground, which didst weaken the nations."

First of all, the word *heaven* here in the Hebrew is *shaw-meh*, meaning "to be lofty"—the sky is aloft, or perhaps alluding to the visible arch in which the clouds move. In other words, this is not the third heaven where God dwells and where the apostle Paul was caught up. If you understand that the tabernacle in the wilderness in the time of Moses was a picture or type of heavenly things. For instance there were two separate rooms and a courtyard. When you entered the gate of the courtyard, you were entering first heaven (which is mentioned in Revelation 21:1, "And I saw a new heaven and a new earth: for the first Heaven and the first earth were passed away"), where the altar of sacrifice and the laver of water was. Like when you first got saved, you went down to the altar at church to accept Christ as your savior, then you would get baptized in water. Secondly, you would enter into second heaven, into the Holy Place where the sevenfold candlestick, the table of shewbread, and the altar of incense was located. Here, the priests ministered, and you were taught the truth by the light of God's word and the bread of Life, and your prayers were offered up in the altar of incense. A very good example is Luke 10:18, where Jesus stated, "I beheld Satan as lightning fall from Heaven." This heaven he was talking about was second heaven, the place in the temple where the priests ministered, just as in the tabernacle of Moses. Remember, Jesus called those Pharisees and Sadducees serpents and vipers (Satan). This system passed quickly (lightning) after Calvary, never to arise again (in other words, fell from heaven as lightning). This was typical of our journey when we first get saved. Third heaven was the Holy of Holies, where the Ark of the Covenant and the Mercy Seat was, separated by the curtain that was rent in two when Jesus paid the ultimate price for our sins at Calvary. In other words, where the Apostle Paul was caught up into—third heaven, where God dwells and which will be our eternal home when the saints are caught up in the Rapture. Although second heaven isn't mentioned in Scripture, it's just common sense that if there is a first heaven and a third heaven, then obviously there has to be a second heaven. This is why this false doctrine on Lucifer and many other false doctrines has been falsely misrepresented throughout the churches.

The Tabernacle of Moses

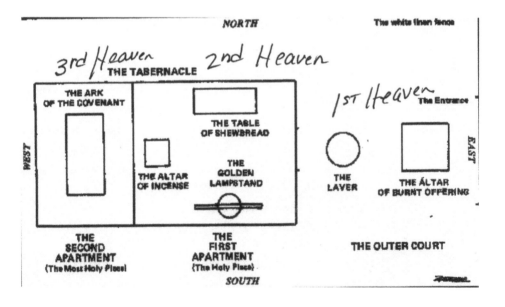

Hebrew 9:23–24 says, "It was therefore necessary that the pattern of things in Heaven [Tabernacle of Moses] should be purified with these; but the heavenly things themselves with better sacrifices than these. For Christ has not entered into the holy places made with hands [Tabernacle of Moses], which are figures of the true, but into heaven itself now to appear in the presence of God for us."

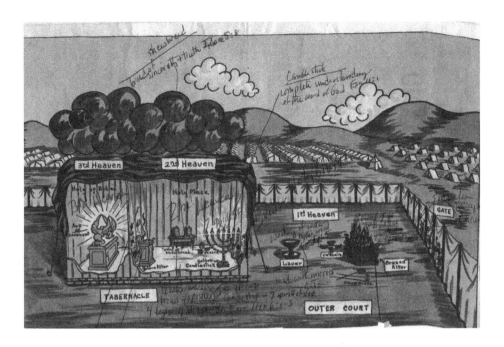

Now this next verse of Scripture totally debunks the teaching that Lucifer fell out of third heaven. Verse 13—"For thou hast said, I will *ascend* into heaven, I will exalt my throne (Nebuchadnezzar's throne) above the stars of God."

The church teaches that Lucifer fell out of (descended from) heaven. Got a problem here. Lucifer said "I will *ascend* into heaven." That means he was on earth or ground, not in heaven. This verse alone completely destroys this false doctrine.

It becomes absolutely clear that this so-called Lucifer is just a man. Let's look at verse 16: "They that see thee shall narrowly look upon thee, saying is this the *man* that made the earth to *tremble* that did shake kingdoms." Do learned men and Bible scholars just skip this verse?

Does it not state clearly that this is a *man* and not a god. Now let's look at Daniel 5:18–19: "O thou king, the most high God gave Nebuchadnezzar thy father a kingdom, and majesty, and glory, and honor: And for the majesty that he gave him, all people, *nations*, and languages, *trembled* and feared before him." Is this not exactly what the verse in Isaiah 14:16 mentioned? This is a *man* that made the earth *tremble*, that did shake *nations*. Is it not perfectly clear that Lucifer is King Nebuchadnezzar only in metaphorical terms? Remember Isaiah 14:4—"Take this *proverb* against the king of Babylon."

Now let's go to Daniel chapter 4, and we'll start at the very beginning in verse 1. "NEB-U-CHAD-NEZ-ZAR the King, unto all people, nations, and languages, that did dwell in all the earth; peace be multiplied unto you." And verse 2—"I thought it good to show the signs and wonders that the high God hath wrought toward me." Verse 3, "How great are his signs! And how mighty art his wonders! His kingdom is an everlasting kingdom, and his dominion is from generation to generation." And verse 4, "I Nebuchadnezzar was at rest in my house, and flourishing in my palace." And verse 5, "And I saw a dream which made me afraid, and the thoughts upon my bed and the visions of my head troubled me." Verse 6, "Therefore made I a decree to bring in all the wise men of Babylon before me, that they might make known unto me the interpretation of the dream." Verse 7, "And then came in the magicians, the astrologers, and the soothsayers; and I told the dream before them; but they did not make known unto me the interpretation thereof." Verse 8, "But at the last Daniel came in before, whose name was Bel-teshaz-zar, according to the name of my God, and in whom is the spirit of the holy gods; and for him I told the dream saying"—verse 9—"O Belteshazzar, and master of the magicians, because I know that the spirit of the holy gods is in thee and no secret trouble of thee, tell me the visions of my dream I have seen, and the interpretation thereof." Verse 10, "Thus were the visions of mine head in my bed; I saw, and behold, a tree in the midst of the earth, the height thereof was great." Note that a tree in the Bible nearly always represents a man or a kingdom. Verse 11, "And the tree grew, and was strong, and the height thereof reached unto heaven, and the sight thereof to the end of all the earth."

Let's stop for a moment and go back to Isaiah chapter 14, verse 14. And compare verses 10 and 11 in chapter 4 of Daniel with chapter 14 of Isaiah, verse 14, which says, "I will ascend above the heights of the clouds; I will be like the most High." Here is the exact fulfillment in of Isaiah 14:14 in Daniel chapter 4, verses 10 and 11. And now remember, this was a proverb against the king of Babylon, which Isaiah prophesied some hundred or so years before Babylon became the first world power.

Let's continue the story of the king of Babylon's dream in Daniel chapter 4, verse 12, "The leaves thereof were fair, and the fruit thereof was much, and in it was meat for all; the beasts of the field had shadow under it, and the fowls of the heaven dwelt in the boughs thereof and all flesh was fed of it." Verse 13, "I saw in the visions of my head upon my bed, and, behold, a watcher and an holy one came down from heaven." Verse 14, "He cried aloud and said thus, hew down the tree." Before I finish this verse, let's look at Isaiah 14:12: "How art thou fallen from heaven [not third heaven], oh Lucifer, son of the morning! How art thou cut down to the ground." Or as in Daniel 4, verse 14, "Hew down the tree." So how do you hew down a tree? You cut it. Sound familiar? Daniel explains to King Nebuchadnezzar in chapter 4, verse 22, as he gives the king the interpretation of the dream of the tree that reaches to heaven. "It is thou, O King that are grown and become strong; for thy greatness is grown, and reaches unto heaven and thy dominion to the end of the earth...which didst weaken the nations!" Now do these verses sound similar to each other? Well, of course they do, because they're talking about the same person, not a god but a king, and cut off his branches, shook off his leaves, and scattered his fruit. Let the beasts get away from under it and the fowls from his branches. Verse 15, "Nevertheless leave the stump of his roots in the earth, even with and iron and brass, in the tender grass of the field; and let it be with the dew of heaven, and let his portion be with the beasts in the grass of the earth." Verse 16, "Let his heart change from man's, and let a beast's heart be given unto him; and let seven times pass over him." This later came to pass, as he was thrown out as king and for seven years became insane and ate grass as an oxen. His body was wet with the dew of heaven till his hairs were grown like eagle feathers and his nails like birds' claws. And at the end of seven years, his reason returned to him. He realized that God rules not only heaven, but rules the kingdoms of men and giveth it to whomsoever he will.

There have been many Lucifers throughout history. Men who have declared themselves to be God. Kings, Caesars, politicians, nutcases, and so-called church leaders. And today is no exception. We have a man who calls himself God on earth and sits in the Vatican, which according to the Bible is blasphemy. Not only does he call himself the vicar of Christ on earth but he also declares that he can forgive sins. Can you imagine a priest can molest little boys during the week and forgive you of your sins on Sunday in that dark little confession booth, and you confess your sins to a *man*? The Scripture says, "Confess your *faults* one to another," not your *sins*. You are to confess your sins to the Lord, not to a *man* who can't forgive your sins in the first place. And that confession booth produces more evil and sexual consequences than can be imagined. Blasphemy! That was the very reason the church, that being the Pharisees and Sadducees, crucified our Lord Jesus Christ. For instance, we read in John chapter 10, beginning at verse 30 through 33: "I and my father are one. Then the Jews took up stones again to stone him. Jesus answered them, many good works have I showed you from my father; for which of those works do you stone me? The Jews answered him, saying, for good works we stone thee not; but for blasphemy; and because that thou, being a man, make thyself God." In Mark chapter 2, beginning at verse 3 to verse 7, "They came unto him, bringing one sick of the palsy, which was born of four. And when they could not get nigh unto him for the press, they uncovered the roof where he was; and when they had opened it up, they let down the bed where in the sick of the palsy lay when Jesus saw their faith, he said unto the sick of the palsy, son, thy sins be forgiven thee. But there were certain of the scribes sitting there, and reasoning in their hearts, why does this man thus speak blasphemies? Who can forgive sins but God only?" And so they were correct. No one can forgive sins but God himself. And no man on earth is God except the Lord Jesus Christ, the only son of God.

I'm going to get off my subject a little bit. But this is very important. There is only one way to test the truth concerning these subjects. Jesus made a very profound and provocative statement when he said, "I am the way, the truth, and the life, no man can come to the father except by me" (John 14:6). This verse alone in these times could very well get you killed; they call it *hate* speech. In the first chapter of

John, verse 1, it states, "In the beginning was the word, and the word was with God, and the Word was God." Verse 2, "The same was in the beginning with God." Verse 3, "All things were made by him; and without him was not anything made that was made." Many of those old reformers and countless millions back in the sixteenth century were tortured and burned at the stake for declaring two major truths. Number 1, the Bible and the Bible only. Number 2, the pope is the Antichrist. The Bible and history itself proves beyond a shadow of doubt that the pope is the man of sin called the Antichrist. The papacy has attempted to change the Ten Commandments the law of God. The second commandment, forbidding image worship, has been dropped from the law, and the fourth commandment has been so changed as to authorize the observance of the first instead of the seventh day as the sabbath. But papists urge, as a reason for omitting the second commandment, that it is unnecessary, being included in the first, and that they are giving the law exactly as God designed it to be understood. In the sure word of prophecy, an intentional, deliberate change is presented: "He shall think to change times and law" (Dan. 7:25 RV). The change in the fourth commandment, "Remember the Sabbath day to keep it Holy" (Exodus 20:8), exactly fulfills the prophecy. For this the only authority claimed is that of the church. Here the papal power openly sets itself above God. How about changing times? Remember Pope Gregory and the Gregorian calendar. He changed times from the Jewish calendar of 360 days a year to the number of years we now observe.

As long as I'm getting off the subject anyway, since we're exposing the Lucifer myth, let's expose another great myth has been taught in the churches for hundreds of years, not only your Catholic and Protestant churches, but also in all the occult churches and secret societies all around the world. And that myth is the myth of the immortal soul. That false doctrine says that when you die, your soul goes on forever, either in heaven or hell. There is nowhere in the Bible that says your soul is immortal. If you can find it, then I'll eat the page that it's written on. Let's just take a few scriptures that prove this doctrine is false. And in this verse alone that I'm going to quote proves beyond a shadow of a doubt that this doctrine is false. Let's turn to the Bible, first to Matthew 10:28: "Fear not them which kill the body, but are not able to kill the soul, but rather fear him which is able to *destroy* the soul and body in Hell [*sheol*, the grave]."

Timothy the sixth chapter, and we'll begin at verse 15. "And which in his times he shall show, who is the blessed and only potentate, the King of Kings and the Lord of lords"—verse 16—"who *only hath immortality* dwelling in the light which no man can approach unto; whom no man hath seen, nor can see; to whom be honor and power everlasting amen." The light, of course, being God the Father, whom no man has seen. And so only Jesus Christ possesses immortality. And this is what God promised us in John 3:16. "For God so loved the world, that he gave his only begotten son. That whosoever believes in him shall not burn in hell forever." Doesn't say that does it. It says that "whosoever believes in him shall not *perish*, but have everlasting life." Or immortality. So that being said, in order to burn in hell forever, you would have to have an immortal soul, and that *cannot* be had unless you except Christ as your Savior. John 14:6 says, "I am the *way*, the *truth*, and the *life*, no man cometh unto the Father, but by me." What is it about that word *perish* that many of the great leaders and scholars and theologians in our churches today cannot understand? Let's look at that word *perish* in the Greek, since the New Testament was written in the Greek language. The Greek word for *perish* is *apoleicho* (*ap-ol'-loo-mee*), meaning "to destroy fully," "to destroy utterly," "to perish." And to me, that's explanation enough. But to reinforce the truth, let's look at some other scriptures. And how about Romans 6:23. "And the wages of sin is death, but the gift of God is eternal life through our Lord Jesus Christ." And this is not talking about the death of the flesh, because we all die in the flesh. This is talking about the second death or the death of the soul. And you'll find many scriptures that talk about the death of the soul. How about Psalm 92 verse 7? "When the wicked spring up as the grass, and when all the workers of iniquity do flourish; it is that they shall be *destroyed forever*." In other words, eternal damnation (Matt. 10:28). In Revelation 20, speaking of the Great White Throne judgment, verse 14 says, "Death and hell were cast into the lake of fire. This is the second death," or the death of the soul. And by the way,

I thought hell was the place of burning fire and brimstone where all the bad people are put on a spit with demons turning you over and over again like a crispy critter. But it says here "Death and hell [Sheol, the grave] were cast into the lake of fire. This is the second death," so we have a little problem here, don't we? How can hell be cast into another burning hell or lake of fire? So what we have been told about hell is also a false doctrine. But it's sure made a lot of people, churches, preachers, and religions a lot of money. Doesn't what I'm telling you make a lot of common sense? Why in the world, as mentioned in John 3:16, would God have his Son beaten, spit upon, and tortured to give us eternal life if we already had it?

Where did this false teaching of the immortal soul begin? In the garden, of course, but also we can go all the way back to Egypt, where if you were very, very rich or a pharaoh, you could buy *The Book of the Dead*. It was primarily a book on how to take the journey to the afterlife. You can still see today the hieroglyphics and artwork on the walls of the tombs in Egypt of the long journey a pharaoh took before he could reach eternal life. My question has always been, How in the world were high priests able to describe the chasms and bridges and monsters they encountered on their journey? I mean, after all, you had to be dead to go there. And how about the book, Dante's *Inferno*. How was Dante able to describe all those tortured souls burning in hell and its seven levels unless he was dead himself. If you think about it, it's rather silly.

I'm going to add two scenarios in Scripture that absolutely no one can prove untrue. The first is 2 Kings 17:17. God sent Assyria and removed Samaria and Israel and replaced them in Halah and in Habor, cities of the Medes, because they left all the commandments of God and worshipped all the host of heaven and served Baal: "*and they caused their sons and daughters to pass through the fire,*" and used divination and enchantments to do evil in the sight of the Lord, to provoke him to anger." So this is why the ten tribes were removed. One of the gods they worshipped was Moloch. The image's arms were heated to glowing red and burned their children alive on them. The second scenario is in Jeremiah 7:30–31. The children of Judah followed suite a couple of centuries later and were punished by King

Nebuchadnezzar and carried off to Babylon. "For the children of Judah have DONE EVIL in my sight, saith the Lord: they have set their abominations in the house, which is called by my name, to *pollute* it. And they built the high places of Tophet, which is in the valley of the son of Hinnom, to BURN their sons and daughters in the *fire*; which I commanded them not, *neither came it into my heart.*" So, folks, we have a huge problem, don't we? The church has been selling us a false bill of goods for centuries. According to them, God must have changed his mind because they still teach today he will pop you into a burning hell forever if you reject Christ Jesus. But since we are not born with immortality, that would be impossible—not to mention that God said it was an abomination and *never* came into his heart. But according to Malachi 3:6, he never changes. "For I am the Lord, I *change not.*"

How about that old "nasty" Satan? Again, let's get the original interpretation of that word in the Hebrew, *saw-tan*, "to attack, accuse"; *saw-tawn*, "adversary," "opponent," "withstand." In the Greek of the New Testament, *satanas* means "the accuser," "the devil," "the adversary." By the way, the word *devil* is not mentioned anywhere in the Old Testament. Only where God mentions to the people of Israel "You worship devils." And the interpretation in Hebrew means "he-goats."

There is a lot of misconception and false teaching on Satan and the devil and, of course, Lucifer. Most preachers, pastors, evangelists, and most all religions in the world do not have a clue as to the real in your face Satan. Let's take a little journey through the Scriptures. And that is because, as I mentioned before, the Word of God is the only book of truth. St. John chapter 1:1 says "In the beginning was the word, and the word was with God, and the word was God. The same was in the beginning with God. All things were made by him; and without him was not anything made that was made. This, of course, is talking about Jesus Christ. For the Word was made flesh and dwelt among us.

The first place that Satan is mentioned in the Bible is in 1 Chronicles 21:1, "And Satan stood up against Israel, and provoked David to number Israel. And David said to Joab and the rulers of the people, go number Israel from Beersheba even to Dan and bring the number of them to me, that I may know it." Now this thing very much displeased the Lord, and the chapter tells how God gave David three things for punishment, and he would have to choose one of them. Now I'm not going to through the story of this whole chapter. But what I am going to do is reveal something in the Scripture that very few, if any, are aware of. And it will definitely surprise many students of the bible. This same story is repeated in 2 Samuel chapter 24. But instead of Satan standing up against Israel, it says, "And again the anger of the Lord was kindled against Israel, and he moved David against them to say, go, number Israel and Judah." Well we've got a little problem here or do we? Simply put, the Lord became an adversary or opponent (Satan) against Israel. So there is absolutely no confusion here. Christians need to stop looking at Satan as some big daddy devil co-equal with God. It's utter nonsense. But to say he doesn't exist at all is also utter nonsense. I'm going to show you who the real Satan or devil is. We're going to defang, dehorn, and dehoof that devil.

Let's look at the true interpretation in the original language from the Hebrew and Greek.

> Serpent = *nahash* (Hebrew)—"hiss, a whisperer, a
>   magic spell, divine enchanter, learn by expe-
>   rience, diligently observe"
> Satan = *saw-tawn* (Hebrew)—"to attack, accuse,
>   be an adversary. An opponent, withstand"
> Lucifer = *hay-lale* (Hebrew)—"brightness, to
>   shine, to make a show, to boast"

Not one of these is a god spirit entity, except of course a man who has a spirit. First Corinthians 2:11 says "For what man knoweth the things of a man, save the spirit of man which is in him? even so the things of God knoweth no man, but the Spirit of God."

A good scripture to start with is in Jeremiah 17:9. "The HEART is deceitful above ALL things, and desperately wicked. Who can know it?" "*Above all things!*" That would include Satan, the devil, etc.

Wouldn't you think Satan would be deceitful above everything? No, the Bible does not lie. How about this scripture? Matthew 15:19, "For out of the HEART proceed evil thoughts, murders, adulteries, fornications, thefts, false witness, blasphemies." Here we have that old culprit again, the *heart*. I know, you're going to argue about Jesus's temptation in the wilderness. So we might as well clear this one up. But first we'll go to Scripture and lay a foundation. Hebrews 4:14–15 says this about Jesus: "Seeing then that we have a great high priest, that is passed into the heavens, Jesus the Son of God, let us hold fast our profession. For we have not an high priest which cannot be touched with the feelings of our infirmities; but was in *all* points tempted like *as we are*, yet without sin." So basically this is saying Jesus wasn't tempted any differently than you or I. So when he was tempted in the wilderness by Satan for forty days, there wasn't some creature standing there saying "Turn those rocks into bread," etc. He knew quite well that he could turn stones into bread by just speaking the words. Just as he could have all the kingdoms of the world as promised to him in 1 Chronicles 17:10–14.

So we are not dealing here with an angel that fell out of heaven. Jesus was tempted to possess all these things without having to endure the cross. Jesus had to resist all the temptations in the wilderness; otherwise, there would be no eternal life for you and me and *all* who call upon the name of the Lord. It was imperative that he defeat that old serpent, the devil, Satan, the very same serpent that tempted Adam and Eve. Did you ever wonder why Jesus was compared to the serpent in the book of John 3:14–15? "And as Moses lifted up the serpent in the wilderness, even so must the Son of man be lifted up. That whosoever believeth in him should not *perish*, but have eternal life." Second Corinthians 5:21 says, "For he [God] hath made him [Jesus] to be sin for us, who knew no sin; that we might be made the righteousness of God in him." Who in the twenty-third chapter of Matthew did Jesus call serpents and vipers? The religious church leaders, the Sadducees, and the Pharisees. "Ye serpents, ye vipers, how can you escape the damnation of Hell [Sheol, the grave]?" He could have just as well have said *Satan*, because they were his adversaries, enemies, opponents.

Was there a literal serpent in the garden that tempted Eve? Let's look at 2 Corinthians 11:3. Paul is admonishing this church when he makes this statement, "But I fear, lest by any means, as the serpent beguiled Eve through his subtility, so your *minds* [or our *hearts*] should be corrupted from the simplicity that is in Christ." Could it have been a real serpent? That's not impossible, but I believe she was tempted no differently than Jesus or you and I. Where was the serpent's dwelling place? In the tree. I guesstimate 95 percent of the times a tree is mentioned in Scripture, it's not talking of a literal tree. Just a couple of examples: Isaiah 55:12, "All the trees shall clap their hands." Psalm 1:3, "And he shall be like a tree planted by the rivers of water." Psalm 92:12, "The righteous shall flourish like the palm tree; he shall grow like a cedar in Lebanon." Trees drop their seeds, and new trees spring up. Man drops his seed, and babies spring up. Get the connection? Ever see a 3D visual of the inside of the brain? If all those veins and arteries don't look like a tree, I don't know what does. And believe me, that serpent still has his home there. Real wisdom in reading Scripture is simply to know when a verse is literal or metaphysical or symbolic. I remember someone saying, it wasn't the apple in the tree, it was the *pair* on the ground. Which to me, although funny, says a lot. Because right after Eve partook of the fruit, God told her, "I will greatly multiply thy sorrows and thy conception; in sorrow thou shalt bring forth children."

As long as we're talking serpents, let's talk about the venom they expel. Many serpents are venomous, especially the two-legged kind that Jesus addressed. The venom these Pharisees and Sadducees spewed out of their mouths was the doctrines, false teaching, and traditions. Jesus said in Matthew 16:6, "Take heed, and beware of the leaven [poison, false teaching, blasphemy] of the Pharisees and Sadducees." Jesus also gave us parables regarding leaven. In Matthew 13:33, "The Kingdom of Heaven is like unto leaven, which a woman [Church] took and hid three measures of meal, till the whole was leavened." That parable has assuredly been fulfilled in our time. Nearly all the Protestant churches are joining together in this Inner Faith movement or ecumenical movement along with the New Age movement and every other occult religions, and making the Antichrist (pope) the chief honcho of this "wide gate" road to destruction. You know, the wide gate Jesus warned us about in Matthew 7:13–15: "Enter ye in at the strait gate: For wide is the gate, and broad is the way, that leadeth to destruction, and *many* there be which go in thereat. Because strait is the gate, and narrow is the way, which leadeth unto life, and FEW there be that find it."

And remember the end of this chapter, verses 21–23: "Not everyone that saith unto me in that, Lord, Lord, shall enter into the kingdom of heaven; but he that doth the will of my father which is in heaven. Many shall say unto me, Lord, Lord, have we not prophesied in thy name? and in thy name cast out devils? And in thy name done many wonderful works? And then will I profess unto them, I never knew you: depart from me you that work iniquity."

Since we are talking about serpents, have you as Christians ever wondered why Jesus's crucifixion was compared to the brass serpent that Moses lifted up in the wilderness? Because the children of Israel complained, God sent fiery serpents that bit them, but if they looked upon the brass serpent that was lifted up on a pole, they lived. John 3:14 says, "And as Moses lifted up the serpent in the wilderness, even so the Son of man must be lifted up, that whosoever believeth in him should not perish [be destroyed forever] but have eternal life." Second Corinthians 5:21 says, "For he [God the father] hath made him [Jesus] to be sin for us who knew no sin; that we might be made the righteousness of God in him."

In other words, sin (the serpent) was nailed to the cross. He came to destroy the works of the devil (the flesh). How is it, when Jesus answered a person about his goodness, he replied, "Why callest thou me good. There is only one who is good, and he is the Father in heaven"? Why would Jesus say that? One reason and one reason only. He was in the flesh, even though he never sinned. The Scriptures says, "The flesh warreth against Spirit, and the Spirit against flesh, these are contrary one to another."

Also, those that love the world, the love of the father is not in them. First John 2:15–17 says this: "Love not the world, neither the things in the world. If any man love the world, the love of the Father is not in him. For all that is in the world, the lust of the *flesh*, and the lust of the eyes, and the pride of life, is not of the Father, but is of the world. And the world passeth away, and the lust thereof: but he that doeth the will of God abideth forever." James 4:4 has "Ye adulterers and adulteresses, know ye not that the friendship of the world is enmity with God? Whosoever therefore will be a friend of the world is the enemy of God." So let's break it down a little. The *world*, the *flesh*, and the DEVIL are synonymous. Simply put, they are *Satan* (*sin*) to withstand—an enemy, opponent, adversary, opposition to God and his commandments, etc. Of course, man has to put Satan in a physical body. Some horrendous scary creature, with a tail, horns, fangs, hoofs, and spits pea soup.

Let's see what the apostle Paul says in Rom. 7:14–25: "For we know that the law is spiritual: but I am carnal, sold under sin [*Satan*—if you read Romans chapters 6 and 7, you can replace the word *sin* in almost every verse with *Satan*, and it will still make sense.] For that which I do I allow not: for what I would, that do I not; but what I hate, that I do. If then I do that which I would not, I consent unto the law that it is good. Now then it is no more I that do it, but sin [*Satan*] that dwelleth in me. For I know that in me (that is in my flesh [*Devil*]) dwelleth no good thing: for to will is present with me; but how to perform that which is good I find not. For the good that I would I do not: but the evil which I would not, that I do. Now if I do that I would not, it is no more I that do it, but sin [*Satan*] that dwelleth in me. I find then a law, that, when I would do good, evil is present with me. For I delight in the law of God after the inward man: but see another law in my members, warring against the law of my mind, and bringing me into captivity to the law of sin [*Satan*] which is in my members. O wretched man that I am! Who shall deliver me from this body of death? I thank God through Jesus Christ our Lord. So then with the mind I myself serve the law of God; but with the flesh [*Devil*] the law of sin [*Satan*]."

Another interesting bit of scripture that has been falsely interpreted is in Matthew chapter 16. After admonishing his disciples about the leaven of the Pharisees and Sadducees (leaven being false teaching, hypocrisy). But they reasoned among themselves, saying, "Is it because we have taken no bread?" They thought he meant literal leaven, which when put into the dough makes it rise or puff up. The true bread of heaven was the unleavened bread of sincerity and truth. The same unleavened bread offered up to God in the tabernacle in the wilderness and the twelve loaves of bread set on the table in the Holy Place. Verse 12: "Then understood they how that he bade them not beware of the leaven of bread, but of the doctrine of the Pharisees and Sadducees." So Jesus was speaking in a symbolic or metaphorical sense, just as Isaiah did when he was prophesying about the king of Babylon or Lucifer in Isaiah 14.

After this he asked them, in verse 13, "Whom do men say I the Son of man am? And they said, some say thou art John the Baptist; some, Elias; and others, Jeremias, or one of the prophets. He saith unto them, but whom say ye that I am? And Simon Peter answered and said Thou art the Christ the Son of the living God. And Jesus answered and said, unto him. Blessed art thou, Simon Barjona: for flesh and blood hath not revealed it unto thee, but my Father which is in heaven. And I say also unto thee, that thou art Peter and upon this rock [by *rock*, Jesus meant *petra*, "a massive stone or rock," which is the statement "Thou art the Christ, the Son of the living God"] I will build my church." Rock? What rock was he talking about? Peter (*petros* meaning "a tiny pebble") absolutely not? God would never build a church on a *man* like Peter, *petros*, a tiny pebble or sand as mentioned in Matthew 7:26–27, which states not to build your house on SAND.

"Cursed is the man that trusts in the arm of flesh." Remember that scripture. You'll find in the Old Testament dozens of times, it mentions Christ is the rock of our salvation. Etc. In the New Testament it's pretty clear. First Corinthians 10:4 says, "And did all drink the same spiritual drink: for they drank of that spiritual *rock* that followed them: and that *rock* was Christ." So you can see a whole false religion was built on a lie. No *man* on earth can be the head of the church. That place belongs to Jesus and Jesus only.

Now you can bet Peter got a little puffed up. After all, he's the one that got it right. But that elation didn't last long. Verse 21 says, "From that time forth began Jesus to shew unto his disciples, how that he must go unto Jerusalem, and suffer many things of the elders and chief priests and scribes, and be killed, and be raised again the third day. Then Peter took him, and began to rebuke him, saying, Be it far from thee, Lord; this shall not be unto thee. But he turned and said unto Peter, *Get thee behind me, Satan; thou art an offense unto me; (or an opponent, adversary) for thou cannot savourest the things that be of God, but those that be of men.*" Wait a minute. If Satan, Lucifer caused a rebellion in heaven, he should know the things that are of God. After all, he dwelt in heaven with the other angels, so *they* say. Just another example of common sense. Now was there a big daddy devil standing behind Peter? Of course not. He was talking directly to Peter—you might say, in his face.

First Corinthians 2:11–4, Paul addressing the church at Corinth, says this: "For what man knoweth the things of a man, save the spirit man which is in him? Even so the things of God knoweth no man, but the Spirit of God. Now we have received, not the spirit of the world, but the spirit which is of God; that we might know the things that are freely given to us of God. Which things we also we speak, not in with the words which man's wisdom teacheth; comparing spiritual things with spiritual. But the natural man (or Satan) receiveth not things of the Spirit of God; for they are foolishness unto him; neither can he know them, because they are spiritually discerned."

So folks, Jesus addressed Peter as a *man* (Satan, the flesh) and would never allow Satan to be the "*rock*" that Christ was to build his church on. "*For thou cannot savorest the things that be of God, but those that be of men.*" So again it's common sense. If Satan fell out of heaven, which most all religions teach, then he would know exactly the things of God. He did indeed fall out of heaven but not third heaven. He fell out of second heaven, which most churches have no knowledge of.

How about Ezekiel chapter 28? Another case of a king or prince exalting himself above God. Let's start at the first verse. "The word of the Lord came unto me, saying"—verse 2—"Son of man say unto the prince of Tyrus, thus saith the Lord God; because thine heart is lifted up [like Lucifer in Isaiah chapter 14] and thou hast said, I am a God, I sit in the seat of God [Sound familiar? The pope in Rome says the exact same thing] in the midst of the seas; yet *thou art a man, and not God*, though thou set thine heart as the heart of God." Now the next few verses, God mocks him. Verse 3, "Behold thou art wiser than Daniel; there is no secret that they can hide from thee." Verse 4, "With thy wisdom and with thine understanding thou hast gotten thee riches, and hast gotten gold and silver in thy treasures." Verse 5, "By thy great wisdom and by thy traffic hast thou increased thy riches, and thine heart is lifted up because of thy riches." Verse 6, "Therefore thus saith the Lord God; because thou has set thine heart as the heart of God." Verse 7, "Behold, therefore I will bring strangers upon thee, the terrible of the nations; and they shall draw their swords against the beauty of thy wisdom, and they shall defile thy *brightness*" (Remember, the Hebrew word for Lucifer is *hay-lale*, "*brightness*, to shine, to make a show, to boast"). Verse 8, "They shall bring thee down to the pit [grave] and thou shalt die the deaths of them that are slain in the midst of the seas" (Remember Luke 20:36? [stated below] Jesus specifically says that the angels of third heaven cannot *die*). Verse 9, "Wilt thou yet say before him that slayeth thee, I am God; but thou shall be a *man*, and *no God*, in the hand of him that slayeth thee." Verse 10, "Thou shalt die the deaths of the uncircumcised by the hand of strangers; for I have spoken it, saith the Lord God."

Let's look at another admonition of the Lord directed at Sennacherib, king of Assyria, who threatened Hezekiah, king of Judea, that he would destroy Jerusalem as he had destroyed all other nations before him and put fear into all of Jerusalem, including the king. After, the king sought for the prophet Isaiah for instructions from the God of Israel. You will hear the same metaphorical language used in Isaiah 14 and Ezekiel 28 regarding the king of Babylon and Tyrus, king of Tyre. This is the rebuke God delivered to the king of Assyria. Isaiah 37:23–24 says, "Whom hast thou reproached and blasphemed? And against whom hast thou exalted thy voice, and lifted up thine eyes in high? Even against the Holy One of Israel. By thy servants hast thou reproached the Lord, and hast said, by the multitude of my chariots am I come up to the height of the mountains, to the side of Lebanon; and I will cut down the tall cedars thereof; and the choice fir trees thereof; and will enter into the height of his border, and the forest of his Carmel." Verses 28–9 has "But I know thy abode, and thy going out and thy coming in, and thy rage against me. Because thy rage against me and thy tumult, is come up into mine ears, therefore will I put my hook in thy nose, and my bridle in thy lips, and I will turn thee back by the way by which thou camest." God sent *one angel* and destroyed 185,000 of Sennacherib's army. But the lesson here is that God used the same symbolic and metaphorical language he used against the king of Babylon and the king of Tyrus. These are nothing more than proverbs and parables used to expose these evildoers. This is why there is so much false teaching regarding the things of God in relationship to the devil, Satan, Lucifer, heaven, hell, and many other false teachings of today. Paul spoke of our day in 2 Timothy 4:3–4 when he said, "For the time will come when they will not endure sound doctrine; but after their own lusts shall they heap to themselves teachers, having itching ears; And they shall turn their ears from the truth, and shall be turned unto fables."

Before we continue, as I mentioned before, let's look at Luke chapter 20, beginning at verse 27. "Then came to him [Jesus] certain of the Sadducees, which deny that there is any resurrection. Saying that Moses wrote unto us that, if any man's brother die having a wife, and he die without children, then his brother should take her to wife and raise up seed to his brother. There were seven brothers and each died and left no children, and last of all the wife died also. So they ask him whose wife will she be of the seven in the resurrection." Verse 34–36, and these next few verses are very important, "And Jesus answering said unto them, the children of this world marry, and are given in marriage: but they which shall be accounted worthy to obtain that world, and the resurrection from the dead, neither marry or are given in marriage: *Neither can they die anymore: for they are equal unto the angels; and are the children of God, being the children of the resurrection.*"

So how do we address 1 Corinthians 6:3? Paul says, "Know ye not that we will judge angels how much more things that pertain to this life." The word *angels* in this verse and several other (1 Corinthians 4:9, 2 Peter 2:4, Jude 6) means in the Hebrew *malawk*, "messengers, prophets, teachers." Ambassadors, kings, not third heaven angels—these angels can be judged and sentenced to death at the White Throne judgment (Rev. 20).

So that would mean, and quite clearly, that Lucifer and the king of Tyrus were *not* gods but angels—yes, not third heaven angels—*angels or gods!* Both these kings died the death of their flesh. In God's heaven (third heaven), nobody dies. Doesn't this make sense? Isn't it rather silly to think that God Almighty couldn't put down a rebellion or control his angels that sinned or supposedly rebelled. And as I mentioned before, then there would be death in heaven, especially since Jesus said that the angels cannot die (Luke 20:36).

Another false interpretation on this subject of the king of Tyre is because of symbolic language God uses such as parables, proverbs, and metaphors, In Ezekiel 28:13–14, this symbolic use of words is more prevalent: "Thou has been in Eden the garden of God; every precious stone was thy covering, the sardis, topaz, and the diamond, the beryl, the onyx etc….the workmanship of thy tabrets and of thy pipes was prepared in thee the day that thou was created [the ability to create tambourines, drums, pipes, or various musical instruments, wisdom for craftsmanship]." This entire verse simply means he was in God's favor, just as Nebuchadnezzar was God's man whom he used to punish the Jews.

So Paul as stated before in Romans 7, "For I delight in the law of God after the *inward* man: but I see another law *in* my members, warring against the law of my *mind,* and bringing me into captivity to the law of sin which is IN my members." Paul didn't say, "The devil [or Satan or Lucifer] made me do it." He made it clear that it was not some outside influence that caused him to sin, but an *inside* influence: *his carnal mind!* Romans 8:6 says, "For to be carnally minded [the mind of the flesh] is *death,* but to be spiritually minded [the mind of the spirit] is life and peace." Verse 7, "Because the carnal mind [mind of the flesh] is enmity [opponent, adversary, Satan]; against God; for it is not subject to the law of God, neither indeed can be." Verses 18–23, "For I know that in me (that is my flesh) dwelleth no good thing; for to will is present with; but how to perform that which is good I find not. For the good that I would I do not: but the evil which I would not, that I do. Now if I do that I would not, it is no longer I that do it, but sin [Satan, Devil] that dwelleth in me. I find then a law, that, when I would do good EVIL is always present with me. For I delight in the law of God after the inward man: But I see another law in my members, warring against the law of my *mind*, and bringing into captivity to the law of sin which is in my members."

How can anything be more clearer? To the general population and most all religions, when the word *Satan*, when the devil, Lucifer, etc. is mentioned, automatically a vision of some two-horned, snake-eyed, split-hoofed, split-tongued monster that spits out pea soup, formulated in the *mind* and throughout history, in paintings, and other imaginative devices invented by the cults, secret societies, and predominantly by the Roman Catholic Church. Do you know what the biggest nation in the world is? The *imagination*. Especially those individuals who have never even read the Bible. Back in what was called the Dark Ages, the Catholic Church would burn you alive if you were caught reading the Bible. Fortunately, men like Martin Luther, Tinsdale, Whittington, and John Calvin, just to mention a few godly men, printed, read, and expounded the Scriptures, proclaiming the truth of the word of God, which began the Protestant movement. And by the way, the two pillars of doctrine of the Protestant move-ment were, number 1, "The Bible and the *Bible only*." Second, "*The Pope is the Antichrist*." And by the way again, *antichrist* doesn't always mean "against Christ," but also "in place of Christ." And countless millions were tortured and burned alive at the stake if they dared disobey or speak out against that Great Whore of Revelation 17 and 18, and it's *God on earth*, the *Pope*.

Pope Pius X:

"The Pope is not simply the representative of Christ, on the contrary, he is Jesus Christ himself, under the veil of flesh. It is Jesus Christ who is speaking, hence, when anyone speaks of the Pope, it is not necessary to examine, but to obey.

"And there was given unto him a mouth speaking great things and blasphemies." (Revelation 13:5)

(Page 15 Jan. 1, 1895, Evangelical Christendom)

The Pope has power to change times, to abrogate laws, and to dispense with all things, even the precepts of Christ.

"And he changeth the times and the seasons." (Daniel 2:21)

(The Pope can modify divine law) Decretal De Translatic Espiscop, Cop, Ferraris Ecclesiastical Dictionary).

It must always be clear, the one, holy, Catholic and apostolic universal church is not the sister, but the Mother of all churches.

MYSTERY BABYLON THE GREAT, THE MOTHER OF HARIOTS. (Revelation 17:5)

(Cardinal Ratzinger, Sept. 4, 2000, "The Independent")

A dragon is on the Papal Crest in the Vatican Museum. Latin; Vatis=diviner, Can=serpent. VATICAN=Diving Serpent

On the Catholic crucifix, is the initials INRI. I=Iustum, N=Necar, R=Reges, I=Impious. Latin: It is just to exterminate or annihilate impious or heretical Kings, governments, or rulers.

Inscription on the three-tiered miter used for the inauguration of Popes; VICARVIS FILII DEI, (Vicegerent of the Son of God) In Roman numerals, V=5, I=1, L=50, C=100, D=500. Total=666, (Revelation 13:18.)

God has given us an admonition: "Have no fellowship with evil, rather expose it!" Ephesians 5:11.

THE DRAGON

Revelation 12

" And there appeared a great wonder in heaven; a woman clothed with sun, and the moon under her feet, and upon her head a crown of twelve stars; and she being with child cried, travailing in birth, and pained to be delivered. And there appeared another wonder in heaven; and behold a great red dragon, having seven heads and ten horns, and seven crowns upon his heads. And his tail drew the third part of the stars of heaven, and did cast them to the earth: and the dragon stood before the woman which was ready to be delivered, for to devour her child as soon as it was born."

Let me begin by saying that the book of Revelation is full of symbolism and metaphors. Obviously, you're not going to find a huge red (red being the national color of Rome) dragon with seven heads and ten horns running around on planet Earth. Nor was there such a creature running around millions of years ago. A dragon in the Bible represents a nation. Ezekiel 29:3 says, "Speak and say, thus saith the Lord God; behold I am against thee, Pharaoh king of Egypt, the Great Dragon that lieth in the midst of his rivers, which have said, my river is mine own, And I have made it for myself." As the beasts in Daniel represents kingdoms or nations, the great red dragon represents the Roman empire and the Pharisees and Sadducees (the tail, Isaiah 9:15) that proclaimed they had no other king but Caesar and who killed our Lord and Savior Jesus Christ. Seven heads represent seven ruling nations beginning with Egypt, Assyria, Babylon,

Medo-Persia, Greece, Rome, and that seventh head, the Vatican (the Roman Catholic Church) that ruled the world during the Dark Ages for 1,260 years, and shed more innocent blood than all the world wars combined. And you'll find in the vestments of the priests and Pope every pagan symbol from Egypt to Rome (the six heads). The ten horns were the kingdoms that sprouted from the Roman Empire (the Anglo-Saxons, the Alemanni, the Herculi, the Vandals, the Ostrogoths, the Visigoths, the Suevi, the Lombards, the Burgundians, and last of all, the Franks). Nor a woman with the sun wrapped around her and standing on the moon etc. So we must conclude that this is drastically symbolic.

Anyone worshipping or believing there are other gods are calling God a liar, just as the serpent in the garden. And they will have to face the White Throne judgment of Revelation 20:14: "Death and Hell were cast into the Lake of Fire this is the second death" (the death of the soul, the end of death, the end of hell meaning Sheol the grave).

Really? It's time God's people wake up to the truth. Hell is a place man invented. It was never preached by Jesus or the apostles. Hell was never a place; it has always been a condition, or the grave, the pit. As I mentioned before, the fifth parable of Luke 15 and 16, the rich man and Lazarus, is simply a parable about the Jews and Gentiles. *Parable* in Greek means "a factious narrative about life concerning morals." Jonah said he was in the belly of hell three days and three nights, obviously not a burning pit somewhere deep in the earth, especially since he was deep in the ocean.

Deuteronomy 18:9–12 says, "When thou art come into the land which the Lord thy God giveth thee to do after the abominations of those nations. There shall not be found among you anyone that maketh his son or daughter to pass through *the fire*, or that useth divination, or an observer of times, or an enchanter, or a witch. Or a charmer, or a consulter with familiar spirits [demonic spirits posing to be family, friends, relatives etc.] or a wizard, or a necromancer. *For all those that do these things are an abomination unto the Lord*; and because of these abominations the Lord thy God doth drive them out before thee." Think about what these verses are saying in regards to a burning hell that supposedly burns you for all eternity. If this upset the Lord so much to condemn this behavior and call it an *abomination*, and to say God puts people or even children into a burning hell forever is absolutely ludicrous. And yet the majority of churches still preach this false doctrine.

Evil Spirits

Let me start by saying that there is nowhere in the bible that Satan, Lucifer, the devil, commanded an evil spirit to do their bidding. But the Bible does say several times that God commanded evil spirits to do his will or bidding. The first place mentioned in the scripture of Judges 9:23 says this: "Then *God sent an evil spirit* between Abimelech and the men of Shechem."

> 1 Samuel 16:14–15, "But the Spirit of the Lord departed from Saul, and an evil spirit *from the Lord* troubled him."
>
> 1 Samuel 16:23, "And it came to pass, when the *evil spirit from God* was upon Saul, that David took a harp, and played with his hand; so Saul was refreshed, and was well, and the evil spirit departed from him."
>
> 1 Kings 22:23, "Now therefore behold, the Lord hath put a lying spirit in the mouth of all these thy prophets, and the Lord hath spoken evil concerning thee."
>
> Psalm 78:49, here speaking of the ten plagues God sent on Egypt, "And he cast upon them the fierceness of his anger, wrath, and indignation, and trouble, by sending evil angels among them."
>
> Isaiah 45:5–7, "I am the Lord, and there is none else, *there is no God beside Me*: 1 girded thee, though thou hast not known me: That they may know from the rising of the sun, and

from the west, that there is none beside me.
I am the Lord, and there is none else. I form
the light, and create darkness, I make peace,
and create evil: I the Lord do all these things."

It is pretty clear as to who created evil spirits, and evil itself—
"That they may know from the rising of the sun, and from the west,
that there is none [other gods] besides me. I am the Lord, and there
is none else."

So now we know who really controls evil spirits, familiar spirits,
devils—and may I say, not only these, but ETs, the grays, shadow
people, and the like. For instance, when Jesus commanded the devils
to come out of the man in the country of the Gadarene (Mark 5:9)
and asked his name, he answered, "My name is Legion: for we are
many" (two thousand to be exact, see verse 13). "And he besought
him much that he would not send them away out of the country.
Nearby were a herd of swine. So all the devils besought him, saying,
send us into the swine, that we may enter into them." These all do
God's bidding, and he uses them to his own purposes.

But a person can entertain evil spirits and be possessed to the
point he can't deliver himself, or having their consciences seared to
the point God will not redeem them.

Mankind brings that on himself, by worshipping false gods, or
contacting familiar spirits (spirits appearing as a close family members
or friends). So for all those that worship Lucifer, God will send them a
strong delusion (2 Thess. 2:10–11) that they would not receive the truth
but believe a lie. God is playing these elitists, God haters, Masons,
cults, secret societies, and every other false religions (Catholicism,
Mormonism, and all other isms) for a cheap fiddle. Isn't it wonderful
to know that God rules in the kingdom of men? Daniel 4:35 says
Nebuchadnezzar finally realized that "and all the inhabitants of the
earth are reputed as nothing: and he doeth according to his will in the
army of heaven, and among the inhabitants of the earth: and *none* can
stay his hand, or say unto him, what doest thou?"

So who will serve our Lord Jesus Christ and receive the free gift
of eternal life? Or will you follow false teaching, and doctrines of devils

that so abound today in these last days, and heed the call in Revelation 18:4, "Come out of her my people, that ye be not partakers of her sins, and that ye receive not of her plagues." And never forget that she (the Catholic Church, the great whore of Revelation 17) murdered and tortured over 68 million innocent Christians during the Dark Ages. But that will be a drop in the bucket compared what's coming. Surely one must realize that when preaching Jesus and lifting up his name is called "hate speech," we are at the literal door of his soon return. And there will be a literal hell on earth for those God haters and evildoers that will cry out for the rocks to fall on them, because of God's judgments will be worse than the plagues brought on Egypt.

The very reason I'm writing this short but powerful message, is to expose who the devil, Satan, and Lucifer really are. It's time to defang, dehoof, and dehorn that lying image concocted by man himself.

The World, the Flesh, and the Devil

The world—1 John 2:15–16 says, "Love not the world, neither the things in the world. If any man love the world, the love of the father is not in him. For all that is in the world, the lust of the flesh, and the lust of the eyes, and the pride of life, is not of the Father, but is of the world."

The flesh—Galatians 5:17–21 says, "For the flesh lusteth against the Spirit, and the Spirit against the flesh: and these are CONTRARY [Greek *an-tik i-mahee*, "opposite," "adverse," "adversary [Satan]," "oppose") the one to the other: so that ye cannot do the things that you would. But if ye be lead of the Spirit, ye are not under the law [the law of Moses, not the Ten Commandments]. Now the works of the flesh are manifest, which are these: adultery, fornication, uncleanness, lasciviousness, idolatry, witchcraft, hatred, variance, emulations, wrath, strife, seditions, heresies, envyings, murder, drunkenness, revelings, and such like: of the which I tell you before, as I also told you in times past, that they which do such things shall not inherit the kingdom of God." So how could it be more clear? The word *contrary* nails it, which basically says the Spirit and the *flesh* are adversaries (Satan). *So Satan, the devil, is not an individual—period!*

Note: so let me repeat it again. The translations in the Hebrew and Greek does not necessarily designate an individual—a single traducer, accuser, slanderer, adversary, and opponent—but can be a multitude, whether governments, armies, people, and specifically, the carnal mind. And any human being can fall into any of these classifications. So basically, if the entire human race should suddenly disappear, so would Satan and the devil. But unfortunately Satan is alive and well in a greater measure than any time in history.

My great hope is that anyone who reads this writing will have their eyes opened to who Lucifer, Satan, the devil, evil spirits (and who controls them) really are in the light of truth. And that one will truly understand that the enemy is not without but within. When Jesus rebuked the religious element of his day, he called them serpents and vipers, whited sepulchers full of dead men's bones.

Within or *without?* Matthew 25: 3–28 says, "Woe unto you, scribes, and Pharisees! Hypocrites! For you make clean the outside of the cup and of the platter, but *within* they are full of extortion and excess. Thou blind Pharisee, cleanse first that which is *within* the cup and platter, that the outside of them may be clean also. Woe unto you scribes and Pharisees, hypocrites! For you are like unto whited sepulchers, which indeed appear beautiful outward, but are *within* full of dead men's bones, and of all uncleanness. Even so you also outwardly appear righteous unto men, but *within* ye are full of hypocrisy and iniquity."

It all comes down to this. You cannot burn in hell forever because your soul *is not immortal.* And the only way to obtain immortality is through Jesus Christ. And specifically, the Bible states that the soul dies, not live forever. In Revelation 20, at the White Throne judgment, those condemned will *perish* forever (the second death). Matthew 19:28 says, "And fear not them that can kill the body but are not able to kill the soul, but rather fear Him which is able to destroy both soul and body in Hell [Hebrew word *Sheol,* the grave]."

And most importantly, God punished the ten tribes of Israel (2 Kings 17:17) and Judah (Jer. 7:30–31) for burning their sons and daughters in the fire to false Gods which the Lord commanded them not, neither came it into my heart and said it was an abomination. So much for *a burning* hell.

We prove in Scripture that when you die, you go to sleep, period! Like the scripture that says in Acts 2:29–34, David is both buried and his sepulcher is with us unto this day. David has not ascended unto heaven. So your Aunt Sally and Uncle Fred did not go directly to heaven or hell; they are asleep.

The Apostle Paul states in 1 Thessalonians 4:14–18, "If we believe that Jesus died and rose again, even so also them which *sleep* in Jesus will God bring with him. For this we say unto you by the word of the Lord, that we which are alive and remain unto the coming of the Lord shall not prevent them which are *asleep*. For the Lord himself shall descend from Heaven with a shout, and the voice of the archangel, and with the trump of God: and the dead in Christ shall rise first: Then we which are alive and remain shall be caught up together with them in the clouds, to meet the Lord in the air: so shall we ever be with the Lord. Whereby comfort one another with these words."

Acts 13:36, "For David after he has served his own generation by the will of God, fell on *sleep*."

John 11:11, "These things said he [Jesus] and after that he saith unto them, 'Our friend Lazarus *sleepth*: but I go, that I may *awake* him out of sleep.'"

Acts 7:59-60, "And they stoned Stephan, calling upon God, and saying, Lord Jesus, receive my spirit. And he kneeled down, and cried with a loud voice, Lord lay not this sin to their charge. And when he had said this, he fell *asleep*."

I could go on and on. The Old Testament quotes nearly forty times that this king died and *slept* with his fathers. Every king that died slept with his father. So what does that say to us that are alive? *When we die, we go to sleep! Period.* What a wonderful and merciful God we serve. Who even states that he doesn't want any to perish, but come to repentance and be saved.

This is your opportunity to ask Jesus to come into your heart and receive the *free gift* of eternal life, something you cannot earn. "For we are saved by faith and not of works lest any man should boast." My hope is that when you read the truth of the Word of God, when your time comes, you will *sleep* in the Lord; and not only then but when you retire at the end of the day, you'll have restive sleep each night.

An Eternal Burning Hell?—Hell No!

If you believe in the false teaching of a burning hell, then you might as well toss out John 3:16. So if God would toss you into an eternal burning hell for not accepting Jesus as your Savior, then John 3:16 is a lie, especially if He so LOVED THE WORLD. Burning you into a crispy critter for ALL ETERNITY is absolutely absurd. So I'm going to give you two more scriptural truths that will blow this whole fable away that's been taught in the churches for centuries.

1. Every mention of *hell* in both the Old and New Testaments, which mentions *hell* fifty-three times, interprets hell in Hebrew and Greek according to *Strong's Exhaustive Concordance* as the GRAVE!
   - Hebrew = Sheol (the grave)
   - Hades = the world of the dead, grave, hell, pit
   - Greek = Gehenna—valley of the son of Hinnom, a valley in Jerusalem

2. Revelations 20 is the white throne judgment, the final judgment of ALL mankind. Verse 13 will completely dissolve this false teaching. "And the sea gave up the dead which were in it, and death and hell (the grave) DELIVERED UP the dead which were in them." So I guess the fire was put out in an eternal burning hell because obviously, these had to stand before God for the final judgment. And if they were on fire, they would burn everybody else up around them (haha). Silly. It's just COMMON SENSE.

I truly believe the Lord wants to expose the false doctrines that Apostle Paul said in the last days the church would "turn away from the truth and turn to fables before his very soon return," which I also believe could happen in our lifetime.

Tithes—Uh-Oh!

I don't know if the church is even aware that tithes were under the law of Moses. It was never taught by the apostles after Calvary. You won't find anywhere in the book of Acts that they collected tithes. The only time Paul made a collection was during the famine to help the Christians in Jerusalem, and only the book of Hebrews talks about the tithes collected to pay the ministers that ministered in the Tabernacle of Moses. But if you refute the false teaching of tithes today in many churches because the pastor needs a larger jet, he'll toss you right out of the church. And yet the apostles made the statement, "Beware of those that teach that gain is godliness, for godliness with contentment is great gain. What did Jesus say about that? Foxes have holes, the birds of the air have nests, but the son of man hath nowhere to lay his head." I guess Jesus didn't need a larger chariot, since he didn't even own a chariot.

I believe as Jesus said that a house divided cannot stand. Is there anything more divided than the PROTESTANT churches of today? Look at the condition of the church today—pitiful! It certainly isn't united! After all, there was one church and ONE church only back in the days of Jesus and the apostles. Truly the church today is being judged and will bring in the "the Day of the Lord" so quickly it will make your head spin. And we Christians definitely do not want to be around when that happens.

You Shall Know the Truth, and the Truth Will Set You Free

I had a dream that I awoke early and was getting ready to go to work, and it was still dark. I was standing in my underwear, looking across the room at a full-length mirror in a closet. I noticed as I was gazing into this mirror that my height seemed smaller that my normal height. So I went over to the mirror and I froze with fear, one of the greatest fears I ever experienced. I looked at my reflection, and behold, it was *Satan*.

> The forwarding pages contain the only paintings I did many years ago. I just realized how prophetic they were for today. The first three on pgs 45–47 were painted before I became a Christian.—The first painting of the nude figure has the scar on my upper arm just as it is today.—I was depressed with thoughts of suicide. Pg 45—pg 48—a painting of my rebellious nature. Pg 47—The young boy WWII was holding out a cup because of hunger. It was a self image of myself and the cup was emptiness I couldn't fill.—Pg 48. Jesus filled my cup with the life he shed on The Cross. He filled my cup for all eternity never to hunger or thirst again.—He is the only answer and hope for today.
>
> Matt 11:28–30

Nude ? with fire

Hinnie " clouds

Boy with cup

Jesus portrait

AN OFFICIAL ONLINEBLOOKCLUB REVIEW:

What do you know about Satan or Lucifer? A lot of us know him to be the fallen angel who started a rebellion and brought sin to Earth. What if Gary Randall Wallace tells you that that is inaccurate? In this eye-opening, mind-blowing expose, To Hell with the Devil by Gary Randall Wallace, the author attempts to counter this fallacy, explaining its origin from misconceptions in history while touching on why it is a significant problem and points us in the right direction. The existence of the Devil is also questioned, as the author stays true to the book's subtitle by blowing the lid off Lucifer's coffin to reveal the truth.

Reading the book's description in anticipation of the contents here had me extremely excited, and I am sure it will excite a lot of readers as well, and after reading the book, I must admit that the author holds up his end of the bargain in many ways. The first thing readers must know and be prepared for about the book is that it will question many of the deep-rooted beliefs that they have towards, not just the devil, but also key aspects of religion. Therefore, an open mind is required while digesting the contents of this book.

In a book of this nature, the source of information of utmost importance, and Gary Randall Wallace does brilliantly to rely on God's word (the Bible), which forms the basis of everything discussed. The author displays his wealth of knowledge in God's word while he points out and explains several scriptures that I would not ordinarily give much thought to. He also helps us to understand that parts of the scriptures should be read literally and some symbolically, and I can see how failure to understand this has led to misinterpretations of God's word today, especially in Isaiah 14:12.

Are you aware that there is first, second, and third heavens? Are you familiar with the scripture (first Samuel 15:23) that confirms rebellion is as the sin of witchcraft, and did you know there's no sin in third heaven? As I studied these parts of the Bible, I found myself learning a log of intriguing things. I will not further discuss the other shocking information held within these pages of the book to avoid spoilers, but I can assure you that you will be exposed to a lot in this concise read.

ABOUT THE AUTHOR

B orn again–baptized in the Holy Ghost in his living room super-
naturally without the laying on of hands when Gary was twen-
ty-seven years old. Graduated from Pacific Coast Bible College with
a BA theology. Missions director for Calvary Chapel in San Jose,
California

Produced a television program on Channel 2B in San Jose enti-
tled *Victory In Jesus*. Smuggled Spanish New Testament Bibles into
Mexico and passed them out in a small village called El Rosario.
(Later and unfortunately, the Catholic monks went hut to hut and
confiscated them to make sure these poor people did not read the
Word of God.) Later moved to Colorado and signed up with Big Fish
Talent out of Denver. Did some commercials and short film work.
Wrote a screenplay entitled "Nino Cochise." Avid reader of Native

American and Old West books. A devout and passionate searcher for *truth* in Scripture for over forty years. This writing about Lucifer and immortality came through the only vision he experienced. It came in two parts. The first part of the vision came to pass ten years after, at a church called the Body of Christ. The second part of the vision was partially revealed in March of 2020 (the coronavirus COVID-19), which also was a conformation that we *are* in the *last days*.—Folks, the Day of the Lord is very nearer than we ever imagined. Unfortunately, it will not be a pleasant day for God haters and unbelievers.

> Alas for the day! for the day of the Lord is at hand and as destruction from the almighty shall it come. (Joel 1:15)

> Blow the trumpet in Zion and sound an alarm in my holy mountain: let all inhabitants of the land tremble; For the day of the Lord cometh, for it is a nigh at hand: A day of darkness and of gloominess, a day of clouds and of thick darkness. (Joel 2:1–2)

The author believes it is possibly in our day. As in Isaiah 5:20, a day when they "who call evil good and good evil; that put darkness for light, and light for darkness; that put bitter for sweet, and sweet for bitter."